Introduction

Most people will be surprised to learn of Abraham Lincoln's socialist leanings. This is because of the deification of Lincoln and the fact the victors always write the history books.

This small pamphlet was first printed by the communist party in Chicago and they were great admirers of the so-called "Great Emancipator" and made no secret of it.

This edition includes a great foreword by Dr. Boyd D. Cathey which really puts the issues in perspective and offers more evidence of Lincoln's feelings and his association with the leading communists and socialists of the day.

It has been reset in a modern typeface with all the original language intact. Also included are some facts about the author and a brief biography of Dr. Cathey.

Was Lincoln a socialist? You decide.

We hope you enjoy our efforts.

— Frank B. Powell, III, Editor

Little Sermons In Socialism

by
Abraham Lincoln

Culled and Commented on by Burke McCarty

Foreword by Dr. Boyd D. Cathey

REPRINTED BY

The Scuppernong Press

Wake Forest, NC
www.scuppernongpress.com

Little Sermons In Socialism by Abraham Lincoln

By Burke McCarty

Foreword by Dr. Boyd D. Cathey

©2021 The Scuppernong Press

First Printing

The Scuppernong Press
PO Box 1724
Wake Forest, NC 27588
www.scuppernongpress.com

Cover and book design by Frank B. Powell, III

All rights reserved

Printed in the United States of America

No part of this book may be reproduced or transmitted in any form or by any means, electronic or mechanical, including photocopying, recording, or by any information and storage and retrieval system, without written permission from the editor and/or publisher.

International Standard Book Number
ISBN 978-1-942806-38-7

Library of Congress Control Number:

2021946561

Contents

Introduction .... *i*

Contents .... *v*

Foreword .... *vii*

Socialist? 1

I 3

II 5

III 6

IV 7

V 8

VI 9

VII 11

VII 12

IX 13

X 14

XI 15

XII 16

XIII 18

XIV 19

About the Author 22-23

1939 Chicago Communist Convention
Lincoln's image dominates the stage and the arena.

Foreword

Criticism of the historical figure of Abraham Lincoln in contemporary American society comes generally from Southern traditionalists and Paleo- (or Old Right) conservatives, who are usually then dismissed or derided by the establishment Republican Party and the present-day "conservative movement" as reactionary know-nothings, unable to understand the natural evolution of American conservatism.

The new bar, the "red line" for the "New Right," dates essentially from the failure of brilliant Southern scholar, Mel Bradford, to receive President Ronald Reagan's nomination as head of the National Endowment for the Humanities in 1981. Bradford was the epitome of the accomplished and erudite academician, yet his deep-rooted traditional and Southern conservatism disqualified him in the eyes of such "conservatives" as George Will and Bill Kristol. Bradford's worst sin had been that he had harshly (if with laser-like precision and accuracy) criticized the modern icon of the newly-dominant Neoconservatives within the "movement"— Abraham Lincoln.

Bradford's major accusations were that Lincoln essentially "remade" the

American constitutional system, positing "equality" as the country's foundational value and enlarging the ultimate power of the federal government, and, thus, beginning a process of governmental expansion and control that continues largely unabated in our time.

Yet, there is another aspect of Lincoln's praxis and agenda which should worry Americans just as much. It is perhaps the best guarded confidence in American history. It certainly isn't something the dominant "conservative movement" or today's Republican Party wish to acknowledge, much less see debated publicly. Yet, the factual record is there for anyone with initiative and curiosity to see for himself: Abraham Lincoln not only had a favorable opinion of Karl Marx and his writings, but was at times sympathetic to socialist policies and ideas.

A few years back (July 27, 2019) a short article by Gillian Brockell appeared in *The Washington Post*. Titled, "You know who was into Karl Marx? No, not AOC. Abraham Lincoln," the author catalogues the connections between Lincoln and Marx, and the list is — or at least should be — alarming for conservative Americans. (I acknowledge my debt to Brockell's investigative reporting for this foreword.)

In his first annual message — his first State of the Union address — in December 1861 he ends the address with a peroration on what the *Chicago Tribune* at the time called a meditation on "capital versus labor." "Capital is only the fruit of labor," Lincoln elaborated, "and could never have existed if labor had not first existed. Labor is the superior of capital, and deserves much the higher consideration."

Those words could have come almost directly from Karl Marx, but they were spoken by Lincoln. Fascinating, since the sixteenth president was an avid reader of the father of Marxism and corresponded with him during the War Between the States. Abraham Lincoln was not a declared socialist, certainly not in the modern sense. But Lincoln and Marx — born only nine years apart — were contemporaries. They had many mutual friends, read each other's work, and, in 1865, exchanged letters.

During his only term in Congress during the late 1840s, Lincoln became a close associate of *New York Daily Tribune* editor, Horace Greeley. It was through Greeley's paper that the ideas and program of the nascent Republican Party were spread. And these were not just the usual anti-slavery slogans we so often hear today when we read of the formation of the party. Often those positions sounded a great deal like socialism, including proposals for the redistribution of land in the American West by the federal government to the poor and emancipated slaves.

At approximately the same moment in time, across the Atlantic Karl Marx was penning his famous text, *The Communist Manifesto* (1848). The failed revolutionary uprising in Germany had compelled Marx to take refuge in England. Hundreds of thousands of other German radicals immigrated to and took refuge in the United States, settling in places like St. Louis, Missouri, where they would play a critical role in later securing that essentially Southern state for the Union in 1861-1862. According to historian Robin Blackburn, in his volume, *An Unfinished Revolution: Karl Marx and Abraham Lincoln*, Marx even considered immigrating and going west to Texas.

According to Blackburn Marx believed the two most significant things happening in the world in 1860 were "the movement of the slaves in America started by the death of John Brown, and ... the movement of the serfs in Russia."

In 1852 Charles A. Dana, an avowed socialist and managing editor of the *Daily Tribune*, hired Marx to be the paper's English correspondent. Dana had been active previously in the utopian socialist experiment Brook Farm, and he carried his vision of a workingman's utopia with him. Marx, in exile, was a natural fit as a correspondent, and for the next decade the founder of modern communism authored 500 articles for the New York flagship paper of the Republican Party, many of them front-page editorials formally expressing the journal's position. And like other contemporary Republicans, Lincoln constantly read the *Tribune*, and certainly, then, he read and digested the writings of Karl Marx. Indeed, it was the support of the German radical immigrants recently come to American shores and the support of the *Tribune* which propelled Lincoln to the Republican presidential nomination in 1860.

In 1862 Dana left the *Tribune*, Secretary of War Edwin Stanton making him Special Commissioner for the operation of the War Department. Essentially, he became "the eyes of the Administration," as Lincoln called him, with an inordinate influence over the conduct of the War … and over Abraham Lincoln. His opinions were received by the president as gospel, and frequently they mirrored the editorials of *Tribune* journalist Karl Marx.

After Lincolns' re-election in November 1864, Marx wrote to him (January 1865) as representative of the International Workingmen's Association, a group bringing together socialists, communists, anarchists and trade unions, to "congratulate the American people upon your reelection." Marx continues in his communication: "… the workingmen of Europe feel sure that, as the American War of Independence initiated a new era of ascendancy for the middle class, so the American Antislavery War will do for the working class."

The president's response to Marx came by way of his ambassador in London, Charles Francis Adams. Adams declared that Lincoln considered the founder of Marxism to be a "friend" and that he possessed the "sincere and anxious desire that he may be able to prove himself not unworthy of the confidence which has been recently extended to him by his fellow citizens and by so many of the friends of humanity and progress throughout the world." The Union, Lincoln added, derived "new encouragement to persevere from the testimony of the workingmen of Europe."

But this was not Lincoln's only tip of the hat to revolutionary social radicalism. In 1864 he met with the New York Workingmen's Association where he insisted that "the strongest bond of human sympathy, outside of the family relation, should be one uniting all working people, of all nations, and tongues, and kindreds."

Of course, Abraham Lincoln never declared himself to be a socialist, and many of his utterances were likely politically-motivated. Yet, he certainly viewed socialists — the workingmen's unions — as staunch allies in his war against the South. As author John Nichols in his study, *The "S" Word: A Short history of American Tradition … Socialism* (2015), comments about "the left leanings of founders of the Republican Party: … it is indisputable that the Republican Party had at its founding a red streak."

In spite of the current historical legerdemain and outright falsification of history, Lincoln continued to be an icon of the Left after his death. In the early twentieth century Socialist Party USA leader, Eugene V. Debs, saluted Lincoln as a fellow "revolutionary." And in the later 1930s American communists flocked to volunteer for the Abraham Lincoln

Brigade to fight, they claimed, "against fascism and Francisco Franco" in Spain's bloody civil war.

One hundred years after Lincoln's death, in February 1968, in an address commemorating communist W. E. B. Du Bois, the Reverend Martin Luther King, Jr. (reputedly a Republican, like his father) spoke in praise of Lincoln's Marxist connection: "… Abraham Lincoln warmly welcomed the support of Karl Marx during the Civil War and corresponded with him freely. … Our irrational obsessive anti-communism has led us into too many quagmires. …"

Every time, then, a Dinesh D'Souza or Victor Hanson Davis, or a representative of the Claremont Institute praise America's sixteenth president and claim him for the conservative movement, while condemning those old "racist" Democrats, alarms should sound for genuine conservatives.

* * * * *

This new edition of *Little Sermons in Socialism* by Abraham Lincoln, was originally edited by Burke McCarty and published by *The Chicago Daily Socialist* in 1910. Compiler McCarty introduces these excerpts from Lincoln's speeches in this manner:

> "*We do not claim that Abraham Lincoln was a Socialist, for the word had not been coined in his day. We do not claim that he would, if he had lived, been a Socialist to-day, for we do not know this.*
>
> *"We do claim, and know, however, that Abraham Lincoln was in spirit to the hour of his death, a class conscious working man, that his sympathies were with that class, that he voiced the great principles of the modem constructive Socialism of today, and that had he lived and been loyal and consistent with these principles which he always professed, he would be found within the ranks of the Socialist Party."*

Thus, this modern edition takes on renewed interest and offers a cautionary note and demurrer to the current glowing interpretation by mainstream establishment conservatives who have made Father Abraham "the second Founder of the American Nation" when his legacy has meant the terrible decline of a once great nation.

Dr. Boyd D. Cathey
September 4, 2021

LITTLE SERMONS IN SOCIALISM

By
Abraham Lincoln

Culled and Commented on

By

Burke McCarty

Run in *The Chicago Daily Socialist*
in 1910

This little pamphlet should be in the library
of every Socialist speaker and agitator

We do not claim Abraham Lincoln was a Socialist, for the word had not been coined in his day. We do not claim he would, if he had lived, been a Socialist today, for we do, not know this.

We do claim, and know, however, that Abraham Lincoln was in spirit to the hour of his death, a class conscious working man, that his sympathies were with that class, he voiced the great principles of the modem constructive Socialism of today, and had he lived and been loyal and consistent with these principles which he always professed, he would be found within the ranks of the Socialist Party.

— *Burke McCarty*

I

Away back in 1847 Abraham Lincoln uttered the following revolutionary language.

"In the early days of our race the Almighty said to the first of our race, "In the sweat of thy face shalt thou eat bread." And since then, if we except the light and air of heaven, no good thing has been or can be enjoyed by us without having first cost labor. And in as much as most good things are produced by labor, it follows that all such things of a right belong to those whose labor has produced them.

"But it so happened, in all ages of the world, that some have labored, and others have without labor enjoyed a large proportion of the fruits.

"This is wrong, and should not continue. To secure each laborer the whole product of his labor, or as nearly as possible, is a worthy object of any good government."

— (*See Lincoln's Complete Works*, Nicolay & Hay, vol. 1, p. 92).

Isn't it odd that away back in 1847, at about the time Marx and Engels were printing the *Manifesto* in Europe, Abraham Lincoln, an obscure, self-educated lawyer in swampy Illinois, got hold of this central concept of Socialism?

Isn't it strange the "Grand Old Party," which always parades the NAME of Lincoln and rarely quotes the language of Lincoln, has given no attention to this, the greatest thought of Lincoln
— THE RIGHT OF THE LABORER TO THE WHOLE PRODUCT OF HIS LABOR!

We amiably ask Republicans to answer, not US, but to answer ABRAHAM LINCOLN.

(Capitals used are by Comentator).

II

Everyone who reads the capitalist press has noticed how persistently such papers fan international and radical quarrels and urge the necessity of this, or that nation, ARMING ITSELF.

Socialists are constantly urging the workers of the world to unite.

Where did Lincoln stand on this subject? In an address to a working men's association, November 21st, 1864, Mr. Lincoln said:

> "The strongest bond of human sympathy outside the family relation should be one uniting all working people of all nations, tongues and kindreds." — (See *Life of Lincoln* by Coffin, P. 395).

When the workers of the world follow this wise advice of Lincoln and the Socialists, there will be no wars, for after all war is nothing more than one set of working men shooting down another set of working men in order to protect the big corporations.

How many wars would we have if the CAPITALISTS had to do the fighting?

III

Socialists the world over are being condemned for voicing the very sentiments which Abraham Lincoln uttered in his annual message, July 5, 1861:

"I desire to preserve this government that it may be administered for all as it was administered by the men who made it. On the side of the Union it is a struggle to maintain in the world that form and substance of government whose LEADING OBJECT IS TO ELEVATE THE CONDITION OF MEN, lift artificial burdens from all shoulders and clear the paths of laudable pursuits for all; to afford all an unfettered start and a fair chance in the race of life. This is the leading object of the government for which we contend." — (See *Life of Lincoln* by Barrett, p. 266).

No Socialist could put forth our contention more forcibly and concisely than Lincoln does here. TO AFFORD ALL AN UNFETTERED START AND A FAIR CHANCE IN THE RACE OF LIFE ! That is what we are demanding and nothing short of that will we accept !

IV

On June 13, 1836, in announcing his political views, Lincoln went on record for woman suffrage when he said:

"I go for all sharing the privilege of the government who assist in bearing its burdens; consequently I go for admitting all whites to the right of suffrage who pay taxes or bear arms, BY NO MEANS EXCLUDING FEMALES!" (See Coffin, p. 89).

Again he said in an interview at Springfield, IL:

"I am opposed to the limitation or LESSENING, of the right of suffrage. If anything I am in favor of its extension or enlargement. I want to lift men up — to broaden, rather than contract their privileges." (See Herndon, p. 625).

This was said later, when the question of Negro slavery was beginning to stir up the country to a white heat. Abraham Lincoln never deviated nor flinched, when it was a question of human justice. He was ALWAYS WITH THE PEOPLE!

V

Abraham Lincoln strongly voices the position of Socialists when he says:

"No men living are more worthy to be trusted than those who toil up from poverty; none less inclined to take or touch aught which they have not honestly earned."

LET THEM BEWARE OF SURRENDERING A POLITICAL POWER, WHICH THEY ALREADY POSSESS, and which, if surrendered, WILL SURELY BE USED TO CLOSE THE DOOR OF ADVANCEMENT AGAINST SUCH AS THEY, and to fix new disabilities and burdens upon them, till ALL OF LIBERTY SHALL BE LOST! (See Annual Message December 3, 1861).

It is the constant effort of capitalism to place Labor beneath it, in the structure of the government. Capital preaches, and thousands of workingmen believe it, that the whole bottom of the social system would fall out, if the capitalists, the "men of brains" were to step down and out. And so long as the majority of the working class continue to hold this opinion, just that long will they be enslaved.

How many railroads would be built? How many deserts would be made to blossom? How many skyscrapers would be erected? How much coal would be mined? How much manufacturing would be done, think you, IF LABOR stepped down and out?

If labor does all these things, why should it surrender its political power, for it HAS POLITICAL POWER, to its enemy?

VI

At Cincinnati, OH, September 17, 1859, in a speech Mr. Lincoln said:

"I hold that if there is any one thing that can be proved to be the will of Heaven by external nature around us, without reference to revelation, it is the proposition, THAT WHATEVER ANY ONE MAN EARNS WITH HIS HANDS AND BY THE SWEAT OF HIS BROW, HE SHALL ENJOY IN PEACE.

"I say that, whereas God Almighty has given every man one mouth to be fed and one pair of hands adapted to furnish food for that mouth, if anything can be proved to be the will of Heaven, it is proved by the fact that, that mouth is to be fed by those hands, without being interfered with by any other man, WHO ALSO HAS HIS MOUTH TO FEED AND HIS HANDS TO LABOR WITH!

"I hold that if the Almighty had ever made a set of men that should do all of the eating and none of the work. He would have made them WITH MOUTHS ONLY, and no hands; and if He had ever made another class that He intended should do all the work, and none of the eating. He would have made them WITHOUT MOUTHS, and with ALL HANDS!

"Inasmuch, as He has NOT CHOSEN to make man in that way, if anything is proved, it is THAT THOSE HANDS AND MOUTHS are to be co-operative through life and NOT TO BE INTERFERED WITH!" (See Howell's p. 148).

Here is Lincoln voicing the Socialist position in the class struggle! The inherent right of every man to the product of his labor, WITHOUT HANDING OVER TO ANY OTHER MAN ALL OF IT EXCEPT THAT WHICH IS NECESSARY TO SUSTAIN HIS MISERABLE EXISTENCE!

VII

Note the stinging rebuke in the words of Lincoln, to our Latter Day Political Saints, who are advocating a centralized government to be in charge of a few leaders TRAINED for the job!

"If the MAJORITY should not rule, WHO WOULD BE THE JUDGE? We shall be bound by the MAJORITY OF THE AMERICAN PEOPLE; if not, then the MINORITY, must control! Would that be right? Would it be just or generous? Assuredly not! I reiterate, that the MAJORITY SHOULD RULE!"

At present we are ruled by a small Oligarchy of money despots, any three of whom could tie up the wheels of industry of this country in forty-eight hours. Think of it! Ninety millions of people who do all the useful work, owned and controlled by half dozen capitalists!

CRAZY SYSTEM, is it not?

Then, WHY DON'T YOU CHANGE IT?

VIII

In his annual message of July 5th, 1861, Abraham Lincoln expressed the stand held by Socialists when he said:

"WHATEVER CONCERNS THE WHOLE, SHOULD BE CONFIDED TO THE WHOLE— the GENERAL GOVERNMENT." (See *Life* by Raymond, p. 186).

Socialism means everything which is used in common should be owned in common. Socialism means all the tools of industry should be OWNED AND OPERATED BY THE WORKING CLASS.

Socialism demands, with Lincoln, that the necessities of life, mines, forests, fisheries, railroads, telegraphs, street cars, telephones, in fact ALL PUBLIC UTILITIES, shall be owned and operated by ALL OF THE PEOPLE!

IX

It is a remarkable coincidence, that more than fifty years ago the city of Milwaukee listened to what was probably its first lesson in international sympathy, cooperation and brotherhood, and that its teacher was not, an "undesirable foreigner" not a "dangerous Socialist" — a Marx or an Eagle, but a simon pure American, who ought to pass muster with our most ultra American critics, who however taboo all such radical utterances of the great emancipator, who said on this occasion in a speech:

"To correct evils great and small, which spring from want of sympathy and from a positive enmity among strangers, as nations or individuals, is one of the highest functions of civilization." (See *Complete Works*, Vol. 1, p. 576).

Socialism is the great, grand principle which is today rapidly uniting the working class of every nation and pointing out its goal — this same cooperative sympathy which Abraham Lincoln advocated.

X

Again in his Milwaukee speech we hear the gentle Lincoln wax satirical and lash the class-conscious exploiters of the toilers of his day, when he said:

"By the 'mud-sill' theory, it is assumed that labor and education are incompatible, and any practical combination of them is impossible.

According to that theory, a blind horse upon a treadmill is a perfect illustration of what a LABORER should be — all the better for being blind, that HE COULD NOT KICK UNDERSTANDINGLY!

"According to that theory, the education of laborers, is not only useless, but pernicious and dangerous ! In fact, it is in some sort, DEEMED A MISFORTUNE THAT LABORERS SHOULD HAVE HEADS AT ALL! Those same heads are regarded as explosive materials, only to be safely kept in damp places as far as possible, from that peculiar sort of fire which ignites them.

A YANKEE WHO COULD INVENT A STRONG HANDED MAN

WITHOUT A HEAD, would receive the everlasting gratitude of the mud-sill advocates."

The capitalistic papers, prelates and other henchmen of the money power, who give gratuitous advice to the working class, to be "obedient and faithful to their employers, to be religious and restrain themselves" were evidently busy in Lincoln's day and were understood by the keen, far-seeing, class-conscious, working man, as he was, to his dying day, and who hit them hard in his own quaint way!

XI

More than fifty years ago Abraham Lincoln stood on truly Socialistic ground when he addressed the striking shoe makers at New Haven, Conn., when he said:

"I am glad to see that a system of labor prevails in New England, under which laborers can strike when they want to; where they are not obliged to work under all circumstances, and are not tied down and obliged to labor whether you pay them or not. When one starts poor, as most do in the race of life, free society is such that he knows that he can better his condition; he knows that there is no fixed condition of labor for his whole life.

"I am not ashamed to confess that twenty-five years ago, I was a hired laborer, mauling rails, at work on a flat boat — just what might happen to any poor man's son.

"I WANT EVERY MAN TO HAVE THE CHANCE — and I believe the black man is entitled to it— IN WHICH HE CAN BETTER HIS CONDITION."

The above utterance of Lincoln, is the ethical basis of the strike and it is the end for which Socialists are striving. A system which will allow every boy and every girl an equal chance to rise in the world and to better his or her condition!

XII

At Alton, IL, in 1858, in a speech, we again hear Abraham Lincoln voicing a Socialist principle in the following:

"That is the issue that will continue in this country when these poor tongues of Judge Douglas and myself shall be silent. It is the eternal struggle between these two principles — right and wrong — throughout the world.

"They are the two principles that have stood face to face from the beginning of time and will ever continue to struggle.

"The one is the common right of humanity, and the other the divine right of kings. It is the same principle in whatever shape it developes itself. It is the same spirit which says 'You work and toil and earn bread and I'll eat it.

"No matter in what shape it comes, whether from the mouth of a king who seeks to bestride the people of his own nation and live by the fruit of their labor, or from one race of men as an apology for enslaving another race, it is the same tyrannical principle!" (*Debates*, p. 234).

If Abraham Lincoln would give expression to these same words from a soap-box in many places in America today he would be likely to be arrested and jailed. That is what is happening to many of the Socialist speakers who are preaching the identical precepts!

XIII

Away back in 1837 in a speech in the Illinois Legislature, Mr. Lincoln in speaking of the brazeness of the capitalists of his day said:

"These capitalists generally act harmoniously and in concert, to fleece the people, and now that they have got into a quarrel with themselves, we are called upon to appropriate the people's money to settle the quarrel." (See Tarbell, 2 vol., p. 28).

The above shows Mr. Lincoln had a very clear conception of the characteristics of the capitalist class and had no sympathy with them. He was astounded at their nerve. How much more so would he have been, could he have foretold that "Jack-potting legislators" in that same Illinois Assembly some 63 years later would have the gall to band themselves together under the caption of "Lincoln Leaguers" going through the great Commonwealth of Illinois exhorting the people to vote against the

Initiative, Referendum and Recall, as did US Senator "Billy" Lorimer and his "bathroom" conspirators!

Perish the thought!

XIV

On Nov. 1864, President Lincoln gave voice to this prophesy:

"As a result of the war, corporations have been enthroned and an era of corruption in high places will follow, and the money power of the country will endeavor to prolong its reign by working upon the prejudices of the people, until ALL WEALTH IS AGGREGATED IN A FEW HANDS, and the Republic IS DESTROYED !

I feel at this moment more anxiety for the safety of my country than ever before, even in the midst of war. GOD GRANT THAT MY SUSPICIONS MAY PROVE GROUNDLESS!" (See Shibley, p. 282).

The dark clouds of threatening Capitalism, wrung the very soul of Lincoln whose clairvoyant eye saw the great class-struggle which we are in the midst of today. The weight of it saddened his heart. He was planning to avert the awful financial depression which was sure to follow the war by opening up the inexhaustible mineral wealth of the West to the men who had fought the rebellion. The last message he sent just as he was leaving for Ford's Theatre the night of his assassination, as he bade Schuyler Colfax goodbye, was "You are going to the Pacific coast. Do not forget to tell the people in the mining regions what I told you this morning about their development. Good-bye." (April 14, 1865, see Coffin, p. 515.)

(The message was, "Tell the miners for me that I shall promote their interest to the utmost of my ability, because THEIR prosperity is the PROSPERITY OF THE NATION, and we shall prove in a very few years that we are indeed the treasury of the world.")

About the Authors

Burke McCarty, an ex-Romanist, joined the socialism/communist movement in the United States early on with the writing of this pamphlet in 1910 seven years before Russia fell to the Bolsheviks.

McCarty seemed to have an obsession with Abraham Lincoln, also authoring *The Suppressed Truth about the Assassination of Abraham Lincoln* in 1922. In this book the author makes the case for the Catholic Church, the Jesuit Order and Pope Pius IX were all in a conspiracy responsible for the assassination of Lincoln, among other things. Modern historians have labeled this book as nothing more than an anti-Catholic screed.

One of socialism's main goals is to do away with all religious organizations, so man's allegiance is to the state, not God. So this book fits right in with McCarty's beliefs.

Dr. Boyd D. Cathey, retired registrar of the North Carolina Office of Archives and History, is an eleventh-generation Tar Heel. He graduated from Pfeiffer University, earned a Master's degree in American history at the University of Virginia, where he was a Thomas Jefferson Fellow, and earned his doctorate in history at the University of Navarra in Pamplona, Spain, where he was a Richard M. Weaver Fellow. He also worked with the late conservative writer and philosopher Dr. Russell Kirk. He is the co-author of two books and dozens of articles in three languages including his latest *The Land We Love, The South and Its Heritage*. He was chief of staff of the North Carolina Division of the Sons of Confederate Veterans, 2002-2009.

www.ingramcontent.com/pod-product-compliance
Lightning Source LLC
Chambersburg PA
CBHW050336120526
44592CB00014B/2206